THE GREATEST
CLASSICAL
MOVIE ALBUM

For intermediate piano solo

CHESTER MUSIC
(A division of Music Sales Limited)
8/9 Frith Street, London W1V 5TZ

This book © Copyright 1997 Chester Music.
Order No. CH61387 ISBN 0-7119-6681-8

Cover design by Keith Richmond
Music setting by Enigma Music Production Services
Printed in the United Kingdom by
Galliard Printers Limited, Norfolk.

Unauthorised reproduction of any part of this
publication by any means including photocopying
is an infringement of copyright.

CONTENTS

THE MADNESS OF KING GEORGE
Zadok The Priest (Handel)
4

THE PIANO
The Heart Asks Pleasure First (Nyman)
12

SCHINDLER'S LIST
Theme (Williams)
17

SILENCE OF THE LAMBS
Aria from Goldberg Variations (JS Bach)
20

TRUE ROMANCE
The Flower Duet from Lakmé (Delibes)
22

BRIDESHEAD REVISITED
Theme (Burgon)
24

A ROOM WITH A VIEW
O mio babbino caro from Gianni Schicchi (Puccini)
26

OUT OF AFRICA
Adagio from Concerto for Clarinet and Orchestra (Mozart)
28

PETER'S FRIENDS
Can-Can (Offenbach)
33

FOUR WEDDINGS AND A FUNERAL
Wedding March from A Midsummer Night's Dream (Mendelssohn)
38

THE WITCHES OF EASTWICK
Nessun Dorma from Turandot (Puccini)
40

DEAD POETS SOCIETY
Allegro from Water Music (Handel)
43

ELVIRA MADIGAN
Andante from Piano Concerto No.21 (Mozart)
48

DANGEROUS LIAISONS
Allegro from Organ Concerto (Handel)
55

SEVEN
Air On A G String (JS Bach)
60

THE GODFATHER III
Intermezzo from Cavalleria Rusticana (Mascagni)
62

THE MADNESS OF KING GEORGE

Zadok The Priest
from Coronation Anthem No.1

G. F. Handel
arr. Jack Long

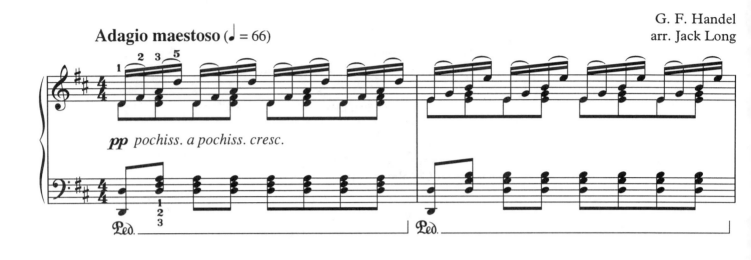

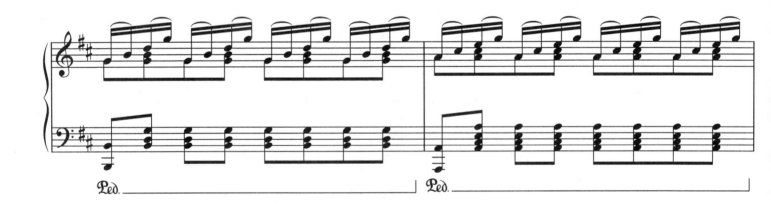

© 1997 Chester Music Limited.
International Copyright Secured. All Rights Reserved.

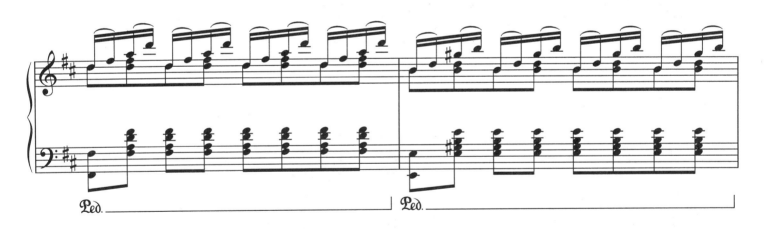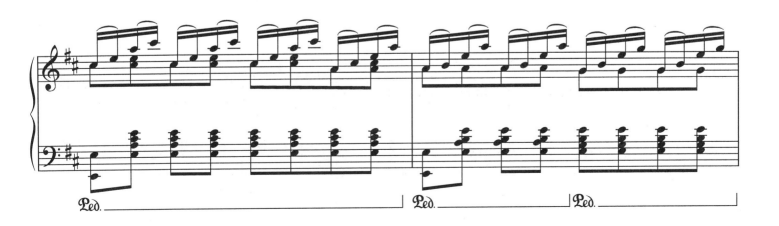

The Heart Asks Pleasure First

Michael Nyman

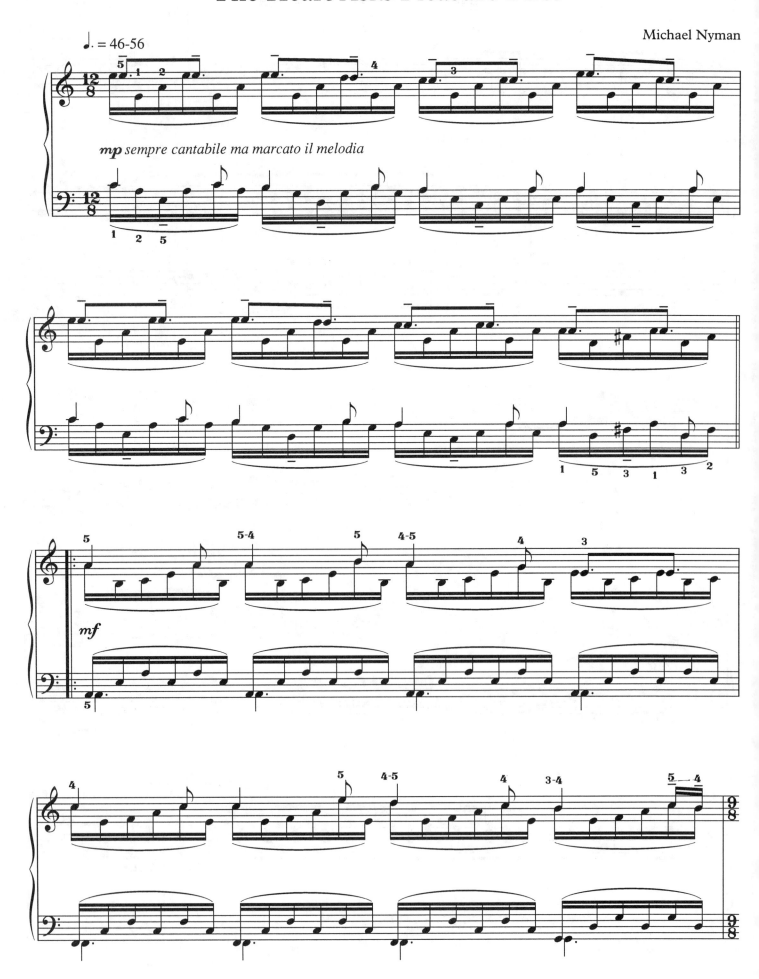

© Copyright 1993 Chester Music Limited/Michael Nyman Limited.

SCHINDLER'S LIST

Theme

John Williams
arr. Jack Long

© Copyright 1993 Music Corporation Of America Incorporated, USA.
All rights administered by MCA Music Limited, 77 Fulham Palace Road, London W6.
All Rights Reserved. International Copyright Secured.

… SILENCE OF THE LAMBS

Aria
from Goldberg Variations

J. S. Bach
arr. Jack Long

© 1997 Chester Music Limited.
International Copyright Secured. All Rights Reserved.

The Flower Duet
from Lakmé

F. Delibes
arr. Jack Long

© 1997 Chester Music Limited.
International Copyright Secured. All Rights Reserved.

Theme

Geoffrey Burgon
arranged by Michael Rich

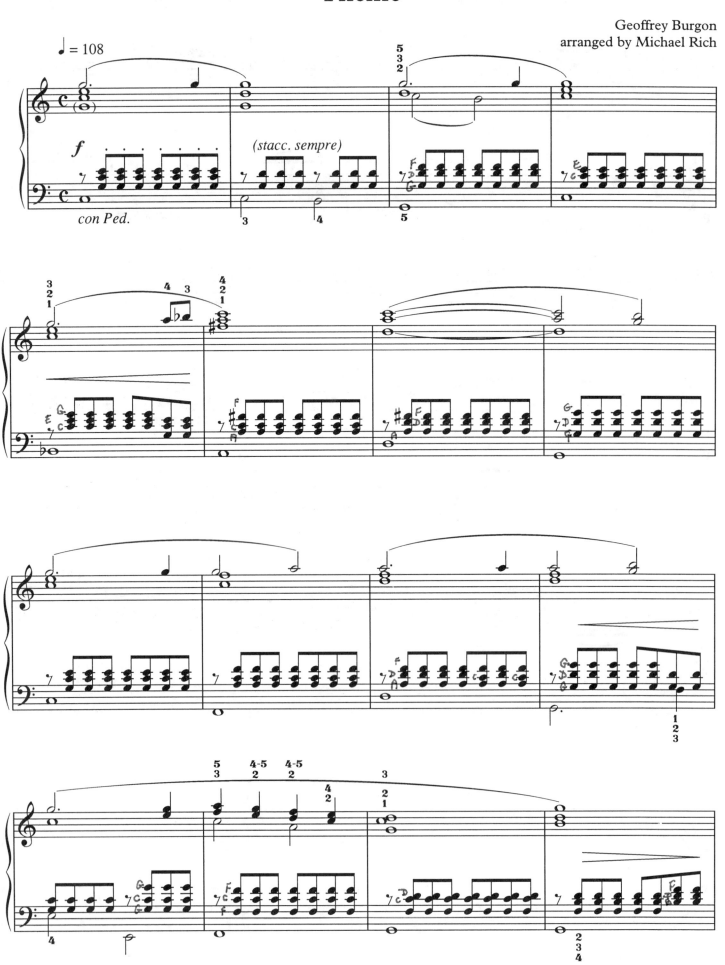

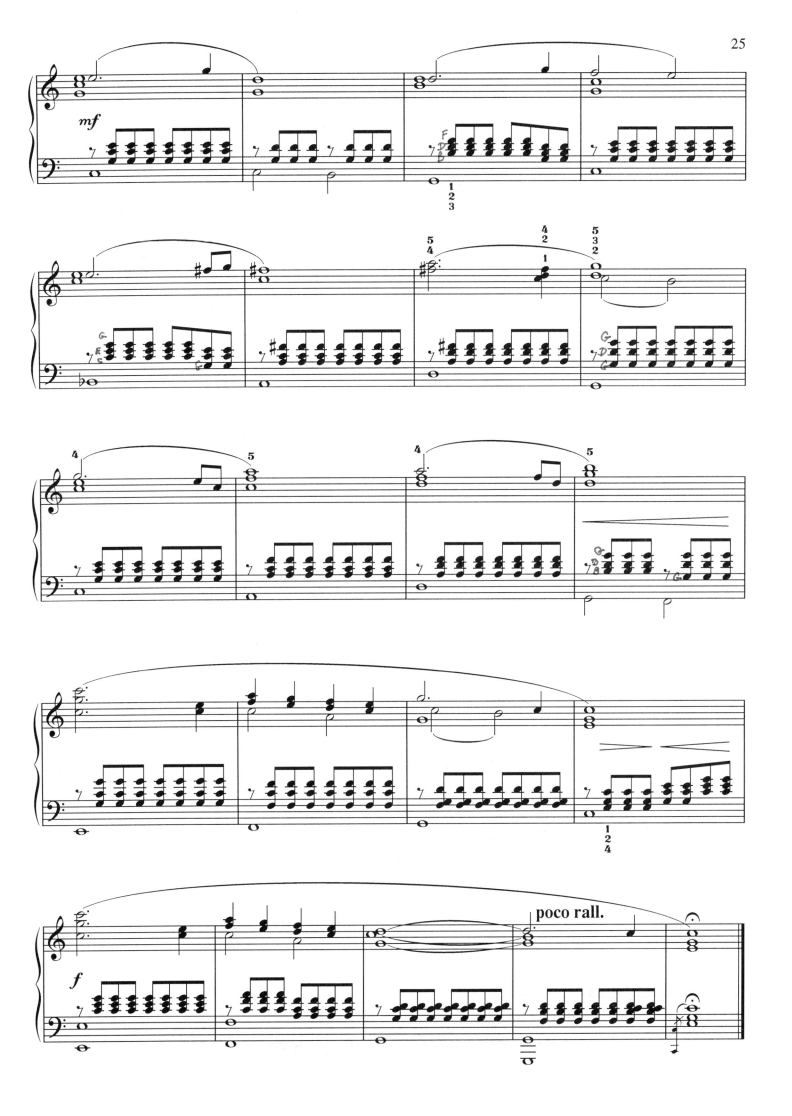

O mio babbino caro
from Gianni Schicchi

G. Puccini
arr. Jack Long

OUT OF AFRICA

Adagio
from Concerto for Clarinet and Orchestra in A K622

W. A. Mozart
arr. Jack Long

© 1997 Chester Music Limited.
International Copyright Secured. All Rights Reserved.

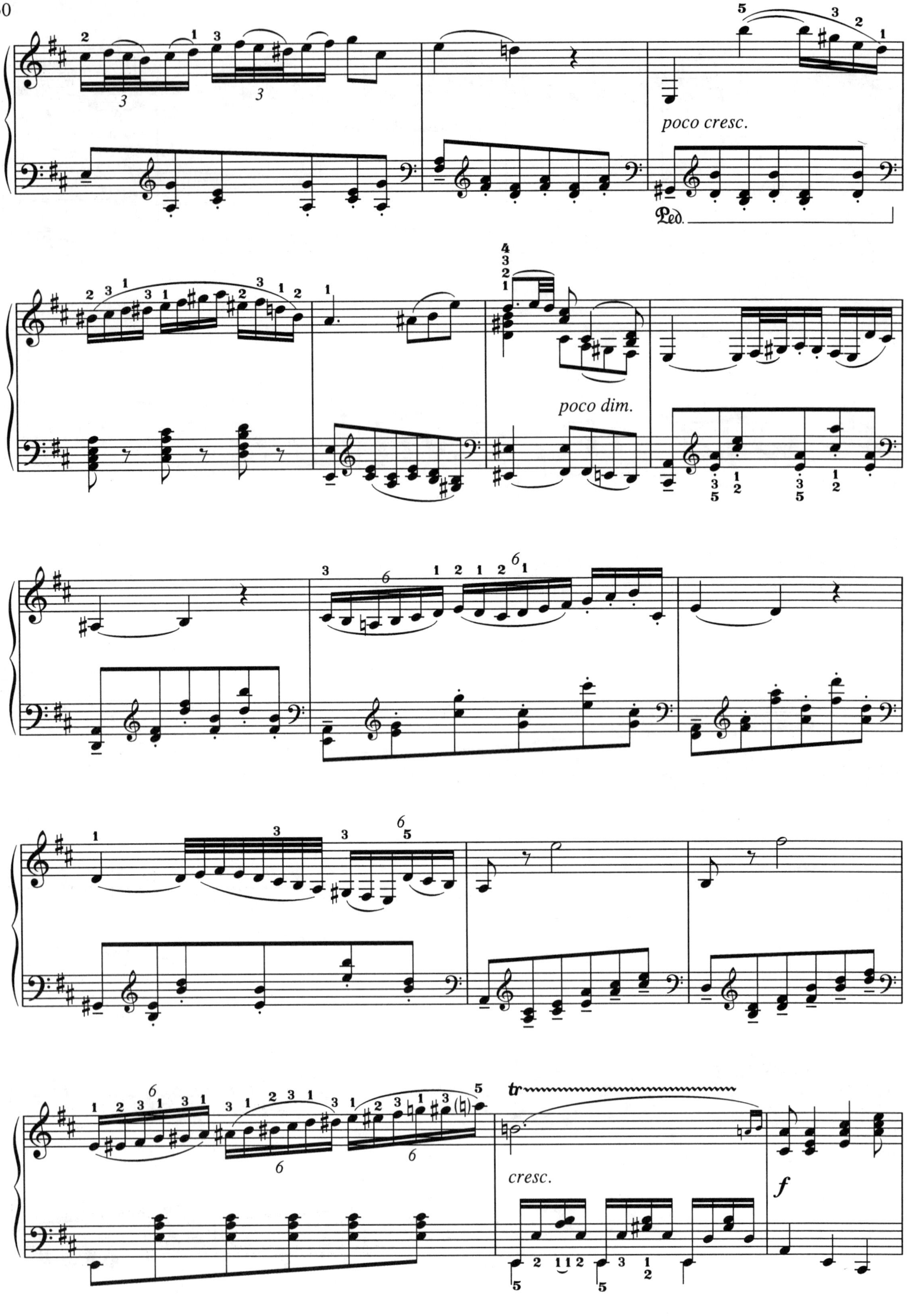
poco cresc.
Ped.
poco dim.
tr
cresc.
f

32

Can-Can
from Orpheus In The Underworld

J. Offenbach
arr. Jack Long

FOUR WEDDINGS AND A FUNERAL

Wedding March
from A Midsummer Night's Dream

F. Mendelssohn
arr. Jack Long

© 1997 Chester Music Limited.
International Copyright Secured. All Rights Reserved.

THE WITCHES OF EASTWICK

Nessun Dorma
from Turandot

G. Puccini
arr. Jack Long

© Copyright Casa Ricordi-Bmg Ricordi S.p.A. Milan. Reproduced by arrangement.

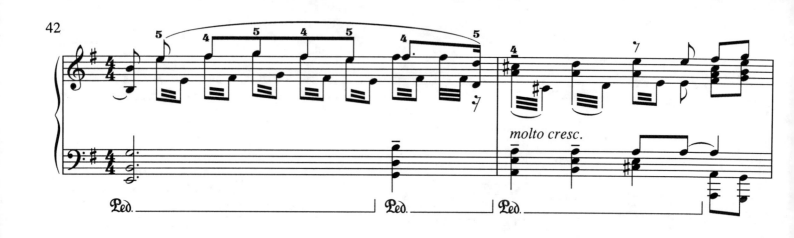
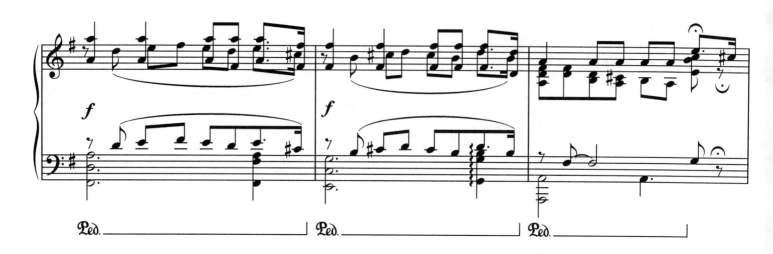
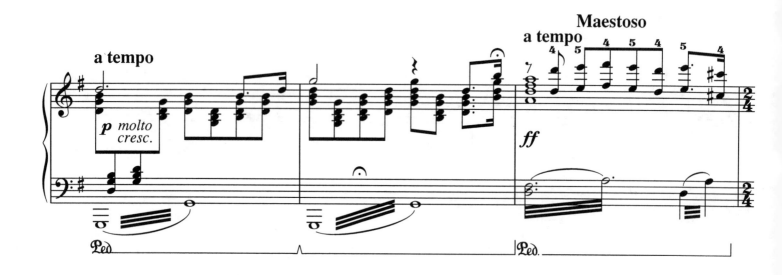
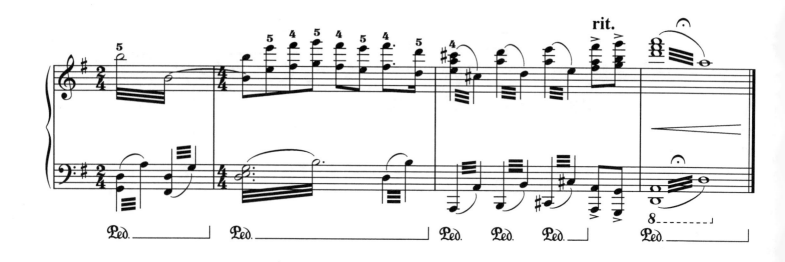

DEAD POETS SOCIETY

Allegro
from Water Music

G. F. Handel
arr. Jack Long

© Copyright 1997 Chester Music Limited.
International Copyright Secured. All Rights Reserved.

Andante
from Piano Concerto No.21 in C, K467

W. A. Mozart
arr. Jack Long

49

50

Allegro
from Organ Concerto in F
'The Cuckoo and the Nightingale'

G. F. Handel
arr. Jack Long

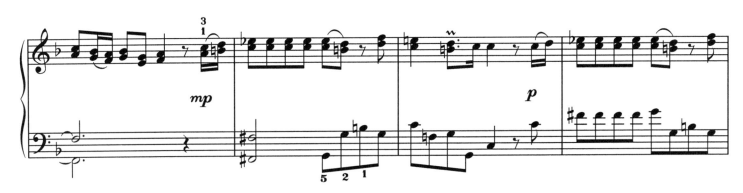

Air On A G String
from Suite No.3 in D

J. S. Bach
arr. Jack Long

THE GODFATHER III

Intermezzo
from Cavalleria Rusticana

P. Mascagni
arr. Jack Long

© 1889 Casa Musicale Sonzogno, Italy.
Ascherberg Hopwood & Crew Ltd, London W1Y 3FA.
Used by permission of International Music Publications Limited.

PIANO MUSIC
AVAILABLE FROM MUSIC SALES

TUNES YOU'VE ALWAYS WANTED TO PLAY CH55834
MORE TUNES YOU'VE ALWAYS WANTED TO PLAY CH58750
Bumper albums containing classical and traditional favourites
in excellent arrangements for intermediate pianists.

THE PIANO (Michael Nyman) CH60871
Original compositions for solo piano from the award-winning
film by Jane Campion.

MANUEL DE FALLA MUSIC FOR PIANO 1 CH61246
MANUEL DE FALLA MUSIC FOR PIANO 2 CH61247
A selection of well-known piano music by Manuel de Falla
including original works and arrangements.

PIANO MUSIC OF SPAIN
A superb three part collection of Spanish piano music featuring the
outstanding composers of the 19th and 20th centuries. Includes
masterpieces by Albéniz, Falla, Granados, Mompou and Rodrigo.
Rose Edition CH61200
Carnation Edition CH61201
Jasmine Edition CH61202

THREE NOVELETTES (Francis Poulenc) CH02193
THREE MOUVEMENTS PERPETUELS
(Francis Poulenc) CH02050

CLASSICAL PIANO SOLOS COLLECTION
A series of ten volumes of classics from the greatest composers
of all time. Essential repertoire for all pianists.

Volume 1 AM91534	Volume 6 AM91539
Volume 2 AM91535	Volume 7 AM91419
Volume 3 AM91536	Volume 8 AM91420
Volume 4 AM91537	Volume 9 AM91421
Volume 5 AM91538	Volume 10 AM91422

Chester Music
(A division of Music Sales Limited)
Exclusive distributors:
Music Sales Limited, Newmarket Road, Bury St Edmunds, Suffolk IP33 3YB.